Behold Thy Mother

Behold Thy Mother

By Ave Maria Dover

Scripture quotations are used from three bible sources: *The Living Bible*, *Holy Bible* (Catholic Family Library Edition), as well as *The Bible's Greatest Stories*, by Paul Roche. The latter is an excellent bible source for good, solid, accurate, and soul-moving scripture reading.

Copyright © 2000 by Ave Maria Dover

All rights reserved.
No part of this book may be reproduced, stored in a retrieval system, or transmitted by any means, electronic, mechanical, photocopying, recording, or otherwise, without written permission from the author.

ISBN: 1-58820-044-2

Printed in the United States of America.

1stBooks – rev. 6/26/00

"Behold"

To look upon with great respect

To regard with attention

Our churches, temples, and mosques do not behold our mothers. They have abandoned our mothers. When you abandon the mother, you abandon her children, sons, and daughters equally.

Beware of False Prophets

Children crossing must be handled
With a delicate hand and an honest soul.

If I may be your guard as you are crossing-
I will hold it close.

If I may see what you feel-
I will hold it close.

If I may mend your sacred heart-
I will be sure it is not left exposed.

For I understand the pain of the lost
And never will I take it for granted.

Stay true- for children are crossing.
Please make sure they stay warm.

-Cristi Daniele

Dedication

To the New Covenant Mary of Nazareth: not a virgin, not docile, not pure. But passionate, courageous, compassionate and filled with the Holy Spirit. She said a resounding "Yes" to God and a firm "No" to the ways of men. Mary had chutzpah!

To my husband of 29 years, Drew. To our five children, Drew II, Kate, Libby, John Paul, and Daniel. It's been a privilege and continues to be.

To my loving mother and father: Kathryn and John Prendergast. Their presence is always with me.

Contents

The Greatest Part Of God 1

Seven Souls, (One American Family) 3

The Root Of All Human Suffering 5

Her Seed, Their Heel. Hers Shall Crush Your Head 11

God's First Covenant Was With The Women Of Israel ... 17

God's New Covenant (God Went To A Woman; God
    Went To No Man) 23

Paul! Paul! Paul! What Have You Done? 49

Modern Day St. Pauls: The Prosecuting Attorneys Of
    Our Children's Souls 53

The Word Game 75

Selective Sin 85

Girls Can't… 93

There Is No Authentic Sexism 99

To the Reader

This book is not for theologians or critics. This book is for the people in the pews and the people who have felt ignored and abandoned by their religion.

This book is short and simple because it is the truth. The truth of what the Holy Bible, the word, says about women at God's altar and the table of life. Now whether you believe in the literal bible or believe it is a book rich in stories with a clear meaning or message, it matters not. What does matter is that people must read the bible for themselves and not accept somebody else's interpretation of what the stories in the bible say or mean. This is especially true for women since the male interpretation of these bible stories have played a major role in the continued degradation of women and their children.

I have read and studied the bible every day now for five years, and this is how I believe the word speaks to women, especially mothers.

The birth of the women's movement began with Eve when she took responsibility for her action while Adam blamed Eve and God. God immediately sensed a major problem for the future of the human race. God at that very moment anointed the women to be the salvation of all human souls. "Her seed their heel" "Her's shall crush your head."

From Eve, Sarah, Hagar, Rebekah, Zipporah, Rahab, Deborah, Naomi, Ruth, Abigail, Bathsheba, Judith, Esther, Mary of Nazareth, Elizabeth, to Mary Magdalene God counted on all these women to save the souls of men. There were and are so many more to name. These women were not virgins, docile, or pure. They were courageous, passionate women, filled with the Holy Spirit. The Jewish, Muslim, and Christian religions would never exist without these women, God's chosen ones, the true spiritual heads of the home. Our mothers are the real churches, temples and mosques. Our mothers are the most sacred beings next only to God.

There is no male headship ordained by God, only by men. It's the simple truth! It's in the Holy Bible. Women must really read the bible because too many men continue to use the bible as a weapon of control and fear.

God's new covenant, the New Testament, a new way, a new movement was almost all due to strong women. God went to a woman to breathe The Holy Spirit into the souls of men. God went to no man. It was Mary of Nazareth who, through her faith, became one with the Holy Spirit. Jesus was flesh of her flesh. It was Mary Magdalene who was Jesus' soulmate and never abandoned him. The men forsook him. Then this repressed soul, Paul of Tarsus, comes along only to undo almost everything the new covenant was about. Paul, not Jesus, took authority and leadership away from women. Paul, not Jesus, took away a wholesome view of human sexuality - two spirits coming together in love, respect, joy, and pleasure, one of the greatest gifts to all of us from God. Paul, not Jesus, brought back control, power, and judgment to religion.

The transmission of spiritual authority was earned by the women of the New Testament, not the men. From the birth narrative to the resurrection, it was the women who stood strong, steadfast, and loyal –not the men. The apostles were able to receive the Holy Spirit at Pentecost only because of the presence of Mary of Nazareth; she was already one with the Holy Spirit.

The most important, astounding and revolutionary fact about the life of Jesus was He made clear the full inclusion and equality of women. Making women your peers was unheard of in first century Judaism. Not so Jesus. He was a product of His mother. Mary of Nazareth was a teacher of a new faith, a new movement. She had a social justice agenda. The proof is in scripture. The proof is in the life of Jesus, the Son Mary raised.

I believe the exclusion of our mothers and daughters by almost every major religion, past and present, is the root cause of every other oppression. We can not, we must not, allow the world's religions to sit our sons and daughters in a pew and teach them this great lie: "God discriminates against your mother."

This book is about mothers, sons, and daughters. It is about having the courage to be. This book is about hope for the world, the truth about the bible and women and peace for the human spirit.

Ave Maria Dover

The Greatest Part of God

The greatest part of God, the greatest gift from God, is and always has been the feminine aspect of God.

Mary of Nazareth became one with God. She was life bearer and life giver to Jesus. He was flesh of her flesh.

Mary molded the soul of Jesus. Jesus became his mother's son, not his father's son.

God the father was judgmental, revengeful and power-hungry. Jesus was forgiving, kind, and a servant to all people. Mary and Jesus represent the best part of God – that is the feminine aspect of God.

Seven Souls, (One American Family)

In my immediate family there is my husband Drew, myself, and our five children, three sons and two daughters. I am Roman Catholic; my husband of 30 years is Southern Baptist. My children were raised Roman Catholic and also exposed to a Southern Baptist experience.

Yes, we are seven "Christian" souls, but wait! Four of us are not fully accepted by either of these religions. Four of us are not equally accepted at God's altar. Why? How could this be? Simple, three of us are female and one son is gay. This wonderful traditional family is told by most major religions that women and gay persons need not apply. One group is told they are inferior, the other group is told they are evil.

The two forms of discrimination taught by most major religions are sexism and homophobia. Basic rights and freedoms God already bestowed on my daughters and gay son were taken away by men not by God. The bible makes it clear that there is no authentic sexism and that homosexuality is not a sin. This book focuses on the real culture of death, sexism which I believe is the root cause of all other discrimination.

THE ROOT OF ALL HUMAN SUFFERING

Every society, every community, every civilization is born of a religion. The world's religions are the nucleus of every society. The evolution of a civilization comes from the religion. The degradation of women is deeply rooted in theology. The continued male interpretation of the bible and koran give root cause to sexism throughout the world.

So keeping this in mind: I believe the root of all human suffering is the world's religions' exclusion of our mothers from God's altar, past and present.

This is and has been the greatest sin of every society, the greatest sin of our world. To exclude women at God's altar is the greatest violation against God. The bible makes it clear. There was never any male headship established or ordained by God, only by man. We will always have racism, ethnic cleansing, hate, and intolerance. We will always have oppression of our children's souls! All in the name of God. Why? Because most of the world's religions continue to teach our sons and daughters that God is prejudiced against our mothers. Yes, God discriminates against women. Your mother is not welcome at God's altar. She is inferior. Your mother is second class in the eyes of God. If we believe God discriminates against our own mothers and sisters then there is no hope. People can always find reason for wars, racism, ethnic cleansing, and homophobia -and all in the name of God. Sexism is the root of all human suffering.

Hope for our children will only come if mothers strike at this injustice. To remain passive, timid, or complacent to the greatest injustice we have placed upon our children's souls is to continue to allow the root of all human suffering, to fan the fires of all other oppressions. Wars, poverty, slavery, racism, ethnic cleansing, and homophobia will continue to be nourished by the great mortal sin of sexism.

Mothers must love their children, sons, and daughters equally. We must seek to change the world or our children now and later will continue to suffer the consequences of an unstable world led by too many unstable men.

As long as men keep repeating the history of intolerance and judgment and the world continues to groan in pain and confusion for our children, so must mothers continue the struggle. The next generation must be women, desperately seeking a vision that ensures acceptance and peace. This vision has already been given to women and ordained by God.

The vision that women are the spiritual head of the family, that mothers are their children's teacher. To teach our children that in order to love God, you must always place humanity above all religious, social, and political laws. We must let our children be who they must, but always with a passion for life and a compassion for all human souls. Our children must know total affirmation comes from God, not any man.

Make no mistake about it, mothers are the anointed ones; mothers are the chosen ones. Mothers are the salvation of all human souls - as God so intended. Yet Christian fundamentalists, Roman Catholics, orthodox Jews, and conservative Muslims continue to teach and embrace the real culture of death, the great cancer of sexism that permeates the very soul of humanity and God.

Our churches, temples, and mosques do not behold our mothers. They do not behold our children. Our churches, temples, and mosques have abandoned our mothers. When you abandon the mother, a woman, you abandon the children, sons, and daughters equally. The devastation on humanity is so great in all fabrics of our society, no matter how many political or social advances women make, be it President, Secretary of State, Prime Minister, Flight Commander, World Cup winners, or Attorney General, it matters not. We will never be whole human beings until we stand equal to men at God's altar; only then will we be equal at the table of life.

Church teachings have made peer relationships between women and men impossible. The children are the victims of these teachings as they watch their mother and father struggle through years of unnecessary verbal, and sometimes physical, combat. The loneliness, hopelessness, and despair felt by millions of women, men, and their children is like a great disease that continues to infect societies throughout the world. This does not build strong families. Exclusion is separation, and separation is devastation for all involved.

Women are responsible for the whole of society. Mothers hold the key to the doors of peace for our sons and daughters. Neither politics nor religions have access to this key, for it is housed in a mother's heart and soul. The greatest responsibility of being a mother is knowing we are responsible for what goes on in the world. If our children continue to suffer at the hands of religions and governments that result in a failed society, then we as mothers have failed our children.

Women are God's warriors, and our weapon is peaceful and simple. We must teach our children well.

Say:

no to sexism

no to racism

no to ethnic cleansing

no to homophobia

no to wars

no to poverty

no to hate and intolerance

no to judgment.

And a firm "No" to any father, brother, priest, minister, or rabbi that would teach our children different from this.

Yes women, a mother is the head of the family. Life bearer, life giver, and molder of her child's soul. First teacher, first authority figure. She is the anointed one. Our mother's lap is the only church, temple, or mosque we really ever need. Yes it is here at the mother's knee our sons and daughters receive the Holy Spirit as she nourishes her child's soul with the food of tolerance, acceptance, knowledge, love, forgiveness, and peace.

God is within every living soul. Every child is our child.

God's heart broke the day men excluded women from the altar because that was the day men excluded God. This is the root of all human suffering.

HER SEED, THEIR HEEL. HERS SHALL CRUSH YOUR HEAD

Women should not be uncomfortable with the way women figure in the bible. It's with man's interpretation of women in the bible that women should be outraged. God is outraged at man's biblical interpretation and outright oppression of women. God knows the truth. After all, it was God who respected Eve for taking responsibility for sin. God had to be picked off the floor of heaven when Adam, taking no responsibility for sin, pointed his finger at God and said, "It was the woman you made my partner. She gave me fruit from the tree" (Gen. 3:12). God trusted Eve. Between sin and the women God put hate. "A war between her seed and your seed. Hers shall crush your head and yours lie in wait for their heel" (Gen 3:15). It is clear women will conquer injustice. Her seed and their heel. Their heel is the women's children, her mission, to raise the children she chooses to have to conquer injustice, to stamp out the evil ways of too many men who take no responsibility for their sins against God and humanity. The woman is the spiritual head of the family ordained and anointed by God from the beginning.

The great sin was not eating the fruit from the tree. Rather, the greatest of all sins, then and now, is blaming God and women. "God saw that everything created was supremely good" (Gen. 1:31), yet Adam blamed God for creating women. Adam and Eve, the fall story, and the male interpretation deeply rooted in the world's religions has played a massive role in the continued second class status of women at God's altar and degradation of all women at the table of life. God was and is devastated. God knew Eve and women to come and their children were in for a rough ride. Man wanted to judge, control, and be master of God, women, and children. God created all of us to be free, make our own choices, and take responsibility for those choices. A man can only be master of women and children if we allow it. When God said to Eve, "Yet you will yearn for your husband who will be your master" (Gen. 3:16), God knew to be master of anyone was the great sin and women must conquer it. Women continue to allow the men in their lives to be their masters with judgment, control, and power. God is still waiting for us to acknowledge Mary of Nazareth properly; due to her faith and action, she and her seed, Jesus, said a firm "No" to the ways of men. Yet we continue the degradation of our mothers, sisters, and daughters at God's altar. God gave the women a mission. God gave the women the power. God gave the women the weapon to undo all Adam and the sons of Adam have done to humanity. The mother and child are the warriors of humanity's salvation. We can and must change the hearts of men and the world. We can teach, mold, and breathe the Holy Spirit into a child's soul. Only then can men and women evolve together and make a peer relationship possible for a healthy peaceful world.

If men continue to refuse to evolve and women continue to accept their status at God's altar, then our father's, brother's, and son's souls will also continue to be shackled. To Adam, God said, "The very soil is cursed because of you and you shall garner from it in toil all the days of your life. It will reward you with thorns and thistles and you will eat the weeds of the field. In the sweat of your brow shall you eat your bread until the day you go back to the earth from which you were taken!" (Gen. 3:17-19) I would say God was really disappointed with Adam, but not so much with Eve. The God of Abraham, Isaac, and Jacob is equally the God of Sarah, Hagar, Rebecca, and Leah.

Without these strong, courageous faith-filled Jewish women, and many after them, the children of Israel were doomed to failure. Let's not forget that God rejected Abraham and Hagar's first born son, Ishmael, to establish a covenant. God wanted Sarah's first born, Isaac. God said to Abraham: "I shall bless her and give you a son by her, and I shall bless him too. She is to be the mother of nations, and out of her shall issue reigning kings" (Gen. 17:16). God seemed more interested that a covenant be established through Sarah rather than Abraham, or his first born, Ishmael, would have been the covenant bearer.

If we are women of faith, if we truly love God and our children, then we must really read the bible and see the truth that there is no male headship ordained by God. When we exclude women from full participation at God's altar, we continue to feed the great sin of Adam, degrading God's creation and greatest gift to all the world, our mothers. Men must realize that the full participation of women in every religion will strengthen the churches, temples, and mosques - and best of all, build strong, loving families. As Jesus said, "Do not be afraid." Our churches, temples, and mosques must stop being afraid of women. Only then can we stop being afraid of people who are different from ourselves, be that difference color, religion, or sexual orientation. Only then can we admit and celebrate that traditional families include our sons and daughters who choose a different path and a different way to love God and celebrate life, as long as it encompasses a love, respect, and compassion for all human souls, especially one's self, for only then can our children truly reach the hand of God.

I do believe our mothers are the most sacred beings next only to God. I do believe women are the chosen to heal our failed societies. I do believe most failed societies are the product of many religions teaching various forms of hate and intolerance. As mothers, we must take responsibility and fill the pews with ourselves, our children, and a firm message to the world's religions: "You will not be the prosecuting attorneys of our children's souls. You will not teach discrimination to our sons and daughters."

If we love our children, we will let them color outside the lines. We will let them walk different paths and even embrace them for walking two, three, four or more paths until they know "this is it." We must let our children be who they must. No evil ever flowed from a person loving all souls and having the courage to be his or herself.

"Her seed. Their heel" (Gen. 3:15). The mother and her child will save the souls of men.

GOD'S FIRST COVENANT WAS WITH THE WOMEN OF ISRAEL

As in the New Testament, the Old Testament reveals to me a great lack of courage and faith with God's chosen men, not the women. In fact, the women of the Old Testament had to endure chosen or anointed male partners who were cowards, murderers, and even confused. The men were anemic in faith, not the women.

Here are a few examples. Abraham and Isaac (father and son), out of fear, abandoned their wives to the Pharaoh and King Abimelech, because they were simply cowards. They showed a lack of faith and great disrespect toward God and their wives. God rescued Sara and Rebecca. Fear, not faith, ruled Abraham and Isaac. (See Gen. 12:10-20 and Gen 26:6-11)

Abraham and Moses argued with God as if God did not know the right thing to do. Abraham argued with God over the people of Sodom and Gomorrah (see Gen. 18:23-33). Was Abraham more compassionate and wiser than God? Moses pleaded with God, "I am not a good speaker, please send someone else." Finally God said, "All right, your brother Aaron is a good speaker" (see Exodus 4:10-14). Where was Moses' courage; where was Moses' faith?

Now David, the "anointed" King David, "the House of David," he murdered a faithful lieutenant of his army, Uriah, so he could claim Uriah's wife, Bathsheba, for his own (see Samuel 11:1-24). I barely scratched the surface here, but you get the picture.

Most of the women in the Old Testament as in the New Testament reveal to me a great awareness of their faith, courage, loyalty, and responsibility far beyond the men's capacity to grasp or understand.

Here are a few of the women from the Old Testament:

Eve: Her seed, their heel will crush the head of injustice. Adam blamed God and Eve (see Gen. 4:12-15).

Sarah: God blessed Sarah: "She is to be the mother of nations, and out of her shall come reigning kings" (Gen. 17:16). She makes sure Isaac inherits Abraham's position and property, not Ishmael, Abraham's first born. "Do as Sarah says for Isaac is the son through whom my promises will be fulfilled" (Gen. 21:12). It would seem Sarah's seed was more important than Abraham's.

Hagar: She listens to God and her son, Ishmael, becomes a great nation, hence Islam, known as Muslims (see Gen. 16:9-15 and Gen. 21:13-19).

Rebecca: She arranges for Esau's patriarchal blessing to be passed to Jacob. Isaac knew nothing of this arrangement or plan. Rebecca's actions were confirmed by God (see Gen 27:1-40).

Zipporah: She saves the life of Moses through faith and obedience to God. God appeared to Moses and threatened to kill him for not circumcising his son. "Zipporah, his wife, took a flint knife and cut off the foreskin of her young son's penis and threw it against Moses' feet, remarking disgustedly, "What a blood smeared husband you've turned out to be" (Exodus 4:24-26). After this, God left Moses alone.

Rahab: A prostitute with great faith and courage helped Joshua conquer Jericho. She later married a nobleman of the tribe of Judah, and became the great-great-great-grandmother of David the King and, even later, Jesus Christ (see Joshua 2:1-24 and Joshua 6:17).

Deborah: She was a prophet who had great wisdom. She was the judge presiding over Israel who ordered an army of ten thousand to march against Sisery, Commander of the army of Jabin, King of Canaan, who oppressed the children of Israel. Victory was for the wisdom Deborah (see Judges 4:1-24).

Naomi and Ruth: The story of Ruth is probably the first story to point out that the Messiah is not just for the Jewish people, but for Gentiles, as well. Ruth (a Moabite woman), in cooperation with her mother-in-law, Naomi (a Jewish woman), plans to win the heart of Boaz. Ruth and Boaz marry and produce a son, Obed. Obed is the grandfather of David. Of course, God ratifies the women's actions. After all, David is the anointed one. (see Ruth 1:7-22, 2:1-23, 3:1-18, and 4:1-17)

Abigail: A courageous, faith-filled woman prevented David, the anointed one, the king, from shedding "innocent blood in an act of vengeance."

Abigail and her faith saved David. She later became his wife (see I Samuel 25:2-43).

Bathsheba: With the help of the prophet Nathan, she secures the crown from David to her son Solomon. Solomon, "the king stood up from his throne as Bathsheba entered and bowed low to her," his mother (see Kings 1:1-43, 2:19).

Judith: She saved the Jewish nation with faith, prayer, and courage. "Give me strength, O Lord God of Israel," she pleaded. "In this hour of need, come to help my desperate act to save Jerusalem." Judith then killed the Assyrian general by way of his own sword (see Judith 13:1-31).

Esther: She confronts Ahasuerus for the salvation of the Jewish people (see Esther 7:1-10, 8:1-17).

God's first covenant survived more due to the rich faith and courage of women, not so much the men. In the next section, "God's New Covenant," it is clear God recruited women to reverse the standards of the world.

GOD'S NEW COVENANT
(God went to a woman; God went to no man)

God went to a woman, a young Jewish woman, Mary of Nazareth for the salvation of the world. Mary was not docile or pure. Mary was not a virgin all her life. Mary of Nazareth was a fully human, courageous, passionate woman. Mary was filled with the Holy Spirit which made her one with God. Mary was not just an incubator, as many religious men like to tell me. Mary had a choice and she said a resounding "Yes" to God; I will have this child and raise him to challenge every religious, social, and political law that hurts or degrades any human soul. Justice before peace in our children's lives.

Mary of Nazareth would be her son's teacher, authority figure, and role model. Mary was Jesus' mother. He was flesh of her flesh. "Her seed, her's shall crush your head." Mary and Jesus together, the mother and her child, crushed the head of injustice.

Mary of Nazareth, who without her zeal, vision, strength, and bold choice, Jesus never would have been the Jesus we love and honor today. Mary raised this child, this man, this Jesus in first century Judaism to say:

>   no to sexism
>
>   no to racism
>
>   no to ethnic cleansing
>
>   no to hate
>
>   no intolerance
>
>   no to judgment
>
>   no to men's laws for the sake of power and control.

Mary said to God, "Let it be according to your word" (Luke 1:31-38). This required faith, truth, courage, leadership and risk-taking, not meekness, purity, or virginity. God's new covenant is the human face of God, the compassionate face of God, but perhaps greatest of all, the feminine aspect of God.

In the bible, it is abundantly clear that Mary always knew the caliber of her son, Jesus. Jesus was never harsh or disrespectful toward his mother or any woman. In Mark 3 31-35 Jesus is not criticizing his mother or family. Jesus was taking the opportunity to say "you belong to me, all of you. I belong to you, all of you. We are all one in the spirit of God. We are all brothers, sisters, mothers, and fathers. We are one in communion with God." He was not being rude to his mother or family.

Remember, Mary is the mother who "kept all these things carefully in her heart" (Luke 2:16-19).

When Jesus addressed his mother as "woman" as in the wedding of Cana or at the foot of the cross, he is not showing disrespect, rudeness, or impatience. <u>"Woman" in Greek was a term of respect</u>[1]. It could mean madam, mother or even my dear mother. This is a very important fact to remember.

Women, oh yes women, are the souls of Christianity. Without the women, Christ's life would not be understood or celebrated today. In fact, I believe he would have been abandoned. The men forsook him. The women stood by him. From the annunciation to the resurrection, it was the women who were front and center supporting, comforting, believing, loving, and offering courage to the suffering Jesus. The men betrayed, denied, misunderstood, and forsook him. I am sure the women were extremely angry and shocked at the men's behavior toward their beloved

Jesus. I am sure Mary Magdalene, Jesus' soulmate, was furious with these friends of Jesus. I am sure that Mary yelled and screamed at some of these men when she caught up with them or, perhaps pushing and shoving them for abandoning her Jesus! Women, oh yes, it was the women who were filled with the Holy Spirit, strong, steadfast and faithful. Not so much the men.

Follow me on a small but truthful journey through the New Testament. You will see it was the women who gave life to the new covenant from the birth narrative, to the resurrection, to Pentecost. There was never a male headship instituted by Jesus Christ, only by men.

The Birth Narrative and the Visitation or the Annunciation and the Magnificat

Mary of Nazareth and Elizabeth: two women, one very young, one very old, rejoicing in their pregnancies. Their faith was overwhelming. These two Jewish women were fully aware of the their duty to God and their children to come. Mary and Elizabeth knew the power and responsibility given to them by God. They were two

---

[1] *The Bible's Greatest Stories* by Paul Roche, p. 374

warriors plotting to change the world. They knew the consequences for themselves and their sons to be. Mary and Elizabeth, two women in first century Judaism who were willing to rock the boat, take a risk, get involved by teaching their children to be dissidents. Teaching their children to say no to failed societies, to say no to religions and governments that crush the souls of their children. Mary and Elizabeth: two Jewish women, truly the mothers of Christianity.

"Mary set out, proceeding in haste into the hill country of Judah, where she entered Zachariah's House and greeted Elizabeth. When Elizabeth heard Mary's greeting, the baby leapt in her womb, and Elizabeth was filled with the Holy Spirit. 'Blessed is she who trusted that the Lord's words to her would be fulfilled.' And Mary said, 'My soul proclaims the greatness of the Lord.'"

Elizabeth was filled with the Holy Spirit at the sound of Mary's voice, and Mary's soul proclaimed the greatness of the Lord. These two women were filled with the Holy Spirit. Their courage, faith, and knowledge that they were the instruments and means to heal oppression enabled them to make the world emancipatory for all.

Elizabeth said to Mary, "What an honor this is that the mother of my Lord should visit me." Mary responded, "Oh, how I praise the lord. How I rejoice in God my savior!" (see Luke 1:38-50)

Mary and Elizabeth were not just incubators, they were not confused or scared. Mary and Elizabeth were full partners with God, designing the blueprint for peace and salvation.

God awaited Mary's choice, yes or no. Mary gave her free consent. God became one with Mary and Mary chose to become one with God. Her child, her seed Jesus Christ, this man was His mother's son.

The Marriage Feast at Cana

"On the third day there was a wedding at Cana in Galilee, and the mother of Jesus was there. And Jesus too, with his disciples, was invited to the wedding. But the wine ran out and the mother of Jesus said to him, "They have no wine." "Mother, what is that to you and me?" Jesus replied. "My time has not yet come." His mother said to the waiters, "Do whatever He tells you" (John 2:1-12).

Mary takes a no-nonsense attitude here. She's telling us and her son it is everything to you and me and the world. Let's not hesitate. Let's not procrastinate; let's act now. The people are thirsty for God's New Covenant now! Mary knew what her son must do. She cues Him to begin His public life. Jesus' first public act was for his teacher, his mentor, his mother!

"After the wedding He left for Capernaum for a few days with his mother, brothers, and disciples." Now why do you think Mary, Jesus' mother, was following Jesus and his male friends around to weddings and trips to Capernaum? Because Mary of Nazareth was a leader, a teacher of the new faith. She was Jesus' first apostle, not Peter, Andrew, James, John, or Matthew but Mary of Nazareth – his mother, a woman, not a man. Or perhaps Jesus was Mary's apostle? Oh, one more question, who's wedding do you really think this was? After all Mary of Nazareth seems to be the concerned hostess.

The Woman at the Well

This story is so rich in many ways. Jesus crossed gender and cultural barriers here and for the first time tells a person, a woman, that He is the Messiah[2]. Now the Samaritan people were practicing Jews, but had their own priests, temple, and canonical list of scriptures. The Samaritans and the Jews did not like each other. Also, a most important fact to know here is that in first century Judaism, men never spoke to any women in public, let alone discuss religion and philosophy with a Samaritan woman. Not so Jesus.

"Jesus, weary from his trudging, just sat himself down as he was by the well. The time was about noon.

"A Samaritan woman came to draw water and Jesus said to her, 'Give me a drink.' 'What!' exclaimed the woman, 'do you, a Jew, ask me, a woman and a Samaritan, for a drink?' 'If only you knew God's free gift,' Jesus answered, 'And who it is that says to you, "Give me a drink," you might well have asked him for a drink instead and he would have given you living water!' Their conversation continued at length when the woman finally says to Jesus, 'I know that the Messiah who is called the

Christ is coming, and when he comes he will explain all this.' 'I am He talking to you,' Jesus said to her. Just then His disciples came, amazed to find Him talking to a woman. But no one asked, 'What do you want?' or 'Why are you talking to her?' The woman put her pitcher down and hurried into town, exclaiming to, 'Come and see a man who's been telling me everything I have ever done. Perhaps He is the Messiah.' And out they flocked from the town to see him" (see John 4:5-42).

Jesus is clear with his example and message we must break down gender and cultural barriers to worship God in "Spirit and Truth." This was the first time Jesus told anybody that he was the Messiah. Jesus chose a woman.

His first public act was for his mother at Cana and His first revelation that He is the Messiah is to a woman at Jacob's well in Samaria.

As God went to a woman, Mary of Nazareth to breathe life into the New Covenant, Jesus also feels a trust and comfort with women, a level of faith he has not reached with the men at this point in His life. It was to his good friend Martha of Bethany, Jesus said, "I am the resurrection and the life, whoever believes in me, even if he dies shall

---
[2] *The Bible's Greatest Stories* by Paul Roche, p.377

live and everyone who lives and believes in me shall never die. Do you believe this?" "Yes Lord," Martha replied, "I believe you are Christ, the Son of God" (see John 11:25-27).

Martha and Mary of Bethany

Martha, Mary, and Lazarus: sisters and a brother from the town of Bethany. Were they just Jesus' good friends? I think there was more to their relationship[3]. After reading and studying the four gospels for over five years now I am certain Mary of Bethany and Mary Magdalene are the same person. There is no town called Magdalene or Magdala and that was how one usually identified a person: by town or village[4].

So how does Mary of Bethany come to be called Mary Magdalene? In Bishop John Shelby Spong's book, *Born of a Woman*, he points out "Magdalene was derived by Mark from the Hebrew word 'Magdal,' which means great or large." So Mary Magdalene meant "Mary the Great" or "the great Mary." Mary Magdalene was Jesus' friend,

---

[3] *The Bible's Greatest Stories* by Paul Roche, p.396
[4] *Born of a Woman* by Bishop John Shelby Spong, p.196

soulmate, and most likely Jesus' wife. God or Jesus never said that celibacy or virginity was a rule to be holy or become one with God. Paul started that nonsense and The Church picked up the ball from Paul and ran with it. Two spirits coming together in mutual love can be the ultimate spiritual experience. I believe Jesus and Mary Magdalene were a close, loving couple: the greatest gift from God.

Jesus made it clear that women must be involved equally alongside of men in knowledge that will shape religion, which in turn molds a society.

"As Jesus and the disciples continued on their way to Jerusalem they came to a village (Bethany) where a woman named Martha welcomed them into her home. Her sister Mary sat on the floor listening to Jesus as He talked. But Martha was the jittery type and was worrying over the big dinner she was preparing. She came to Jesus and said, "Sir, doesn't it seem unfair to you that my sister just sits here while I do all the work? Tell her to come and help me." But Jesus said to her, "Martha, dear friend. You are so upset over all these details! There is really only one thing worth being concerned about. Mary has discovered it, and I won't take it away from her" (Luke 10:38-42). Jesus recognized Mary's rightful place at the table of life. Jesus had women friends and disciples. All through the New Testament, the four gospels, Jesus boldly proclaims the equality and full inclusion of women. Jesus spoke against divorce to protect women. Women were considered property in first century Judaism; they had little or no rights. Men divorced women for almost any reason. Women did not divorce men. Jesus respected women, loved women, hung out with women, but, most of all, trusted women. Jesus made women his peers.

The most powerful argument regarding the true status of women at God's altar and the table of life is the four gospels. Women must realize this and when they do so, the truth will set them free.

"Six days before Passover ceremonies began, Jesus arrived in Bethany where Lazarus was – the man he had brought back to life. A banquet was prepared in Jesus' honor. Martha served and Lazarus sat at the table with Him. Then Mary took a jar of costly perfume made from essence of nard and anointed Jesus' feet with it and wiped them with her hair. The house was filled with fragrance. But Judas Iscariot, one of His disciples, the one who would betray Him said, 'That perfume was worth a fortune. It should have been sold and the money given to the poor.' Jesus replied, 'Let her alone. She did it in preparation for my burial" (John 12:1-7). Mary of Bethany, also known as Mary Magdalene or in Hebrew, Mary the Great. It was this woman, this Mary, Jesus' partner, soulmate, and disciple who new what was to come. "She did it in preparation for my Burial." Mary knew what she was doing. She loved Jesus and Jesus loved Mary. Just as Mary of Nazareth knew at Cana, Jesus' time had come to begin his public life. Here in Bethany at Martha's home, Mary of Bethany knows Jesus' life is coming to an end.

Let us not forget when Lazarus, Martha's and Mary's brother and Jesus' friend, died. Although Martha ran to greet Jesus when he arrived at Bethany, Mary stayed at home. I think Mary was so overcome with grief at the death of her brother Lazarus and very angry with Jesus for not being there or coming sooner, as he could have. Now Jesus made no move to raise Lazarus from the dead until he saw Mary. Martha ran to get her sister. "He is here and wants to see you" (John 11:28-29). Jesus wants to see Mary. When Mary arrived where Jesus was, she fell down at His feet saying, "Sir if you had been here, my brother would still be alive" (John 11:32). When Jesus saw Mary weeping, He was moved. "Where is he buried?" Jesus asked them. Now Jesus Himself cries and raises Lazarus from the dead (John 11:33-35).

Why did Jesus insist Mary come to Him when the older sister Martha was already present? Why did it take Mary's faith and presence to move Jesus to indignation and tears and not Martha's presence? The answer to this is that Jesus and Mary were partners and soulmates to the end. The women were always at the center of Jesus' movement. Luke is the only gospel that tries to make Mary Magdalene a questionable woman. No other gospel supports or suggests that Mary Magdalene was a prostitute. It was also the women who financed Jesus' movement. "Joanna, Susanne, and many others who were contributing from their private means to the support of Jesus and his disciples" (Luke 8:2-3).

Betrayed and Denied

Jesus was betrayed with a kiss by one of the 12. "Meanwhile, all his disciples had fled." The gentleman, the men, the guys, the fellows, the 12, the boys ran and hid. They forsook Him. Peter denied Him three times. The women did not. They stayed, they wept, they followed. The women believed; they had courage. They had faith.

"Judas walked over to Jesus and kissed Him on the cheek in friendly greeting, but Jesus said, 'Judas, how can you do this, betray the Messiah with a kiss?" (Luke 22:47-48)

"Then Jesus addressed the chief priests and captains of the temple guards and the religious leaders who headed the mob.

"So they seized Him and led Him to the high priest's residence and Peter followed at a distance" (Luke 22:52, 54).

Before the night was over, Peter, "the rock," the leader of the 12, the "first pope," flatly denied Christ three times. A servant girl recognized Peter, "This man was with Jesus." "Peter denied it." "Woman,' he said. I do not even know the man" (Luke 22:56-57).

The Walk to the Cross

"As the crowd led Jesus away to his death, great crowds trailed along behind Him and many grief stricken women." But Jesus turned and said to them, "Daughters of Jerusalem, don't weep for me, but for yourselves and your children. For the days are coming when the women who have no children will be counted fortunate indeed. For if such things as this are done to me, the living tree, what will they do to you?" (Luke 23:28-29, 31)

Jesus' message is clear: Men's hearts are hard to change. No matter what Jesus taught them and examples He gave, especially the lesson at the last supper. "I, the lord and teacher, have washed your feet. You ought to wash each other's feet. I have given you an example to follow. Do as I have done to you" (John 13:12-15). We are to become servants to people – to serve, care, help, teach, comfort, and love all people. But the men failed to understand and still do, especially religious leaders. Men still embrace power, control, intolerance, judgment, and punishment, and the people in the pews have become their servants. The greatest victims who suffer great consequences at the hands of the church leaders are women and their children. Sons and daughters equally feel the sting of poverty, hunger, disease, wars, despair, and hopelessness.

Yes, Jesus addressed the women of Jerusalem and told them to weep for themselves and their children because men would continue to brutalize women's souls and the souls of their children. The state of Kosovo today is a prime example of this. I think Jesus' words to the women are a good argument for contraceptives and women's general right to reproductive freedom. Sometimes the world is so brutal, it is best not to bring a child into this world.

The Foot of the Cross

"Now there standing by the cross of Jesus was his mother, his mother's sister, and Mary Magdalene" (John 19:25). It is at this time that the disciple John shows up and stands by Jesus' mother, Mary of Nazareth. The disciple "Jesus loved," John was the youngest of all the apostles, probably about 16 or 17 years old. Jesus and John had a father-son relationship. His youth and love for this man gave him courage to come to the cross. John was but a young man, beyond himself with grief. "When Jesus, therefore, saw His mother and the distraught disciple whom he loved, he said to His mother, 'Woman, behold thy son,' then He said to John, 'Behold thy mother,' and from that hour the disciple took her into his home (John 19:26-27). Jesus knew John needed His mother, just as Jesus did.

The message and symbolism is rich in meaning. The woman is the spiritual head of the family. The mother and the child are the New Covenant. Once again, her seed, their heel will crush the head of injustice. Mary's courage to change the hearts of men by raising her child to say no to the status quo. Mary of Nazareth had the guts and faith to sacrifice a peaceful life for herself and her children so she could rescue the souls of all children to come. Mary's spirit must be brought into all our homes, empowering women to be responsible, to insist on social justice, to improve society, and to raise our children to carry the torch. This is the New Covenant: Mary of Nazareth and her seed, Jesus of Nazareth.

After Jesus summoned Mary, his mother, and John to the cross, He knew "That all things were now accomplished" (John 19:28). Jesus was now ready to "give up his spirit."

The New Covenant: it began with a woman and her child. The New Covenant was now complete with a woman and her child. Mary of Nazareth, one with the Holy Spirit: she is the feminine aspect of God!

Mary Magdalene, Jesus and the Resurrection

Mary Magdalene never forsook Jesus. This woman was His partner, friend, disciple, and I am sure, His wife. It was Mary Magdalene who went all alone to claim the Body of Jesus. In first century Judaism, not just any woman could claim a body. She had to be his wife. It was Mary Magdalene who anointed Jesus' head just a few days before His death. She prepared His body for burial. Like His mother, Mary of Nazareth, Mary Magdalene knew the caliber of this man Jesus. They were partners in faith, as well as life.

"Now on the first day of the week, Mary Magdalene came early to the tomb while it was still dark and she saw the stone taken away from the tomb. She ran therefore and came to Simon Peter, and to the other disciple who Jesus loved, and said to them, 'They have taken the lord from the tomb, and we do not know where they have laid Him."

The apostles Peter and John checked the tomb and then went home. But Mary Magdalene stayed. She was beyond herself with grief for she loved Him so.

"But Mary was standing outside weeping at the tomb. So as she wept, she stooped down and looked into the tomb, and saw two angels in white sitting, one at the head and one at the feet where the body of Jesus had been laid. They said to her, 'Woman, why are you weeping?' She said to them, 'because they have taken away my Lord, and I do not know where they have laid Him."

This chapter and verse of the Holy Bible always brings tears to my eyes because I feel the love that permeates every love story ever told or written by any soul anywhere at anytime in the history of the world. This is a woman who so loved this man that she needed to see and be near his being. She was devastated and distraught His body was not where she could mourn and say good-bye for as long as she needed. No, Mary would never have forsook Him, even in death.

"She turned around and beheld Jesus standing there and she did not know it was Jesus. Jesus said to her, 'Woman, why art you weeping? Whom dost you seek?' She, thinking that he was the gardener, said to Him, 'Sir, if thou hast removed Him, tell me where thou hast laid Him and I will take Him away.' Jesus said to her, 'Mary!' Turning, she said to Him, 'Rabboni!" which is what Jewish women called their husbands in first century Judaism.

I can now imagine Mary jumping up and throwing herself at Jesus, hugging, kissing, and touching Jesus all while crying and laughing. I am sure Jesus was doing the same. I am sure when Jesus said to Mary, "Do not touch me," He was trying to get Mary to let go of Him so He could talk with her. Jesus was telling Mary, I am still with you. I have not gone to my father. Yes, it was Mary Magdalene Jesus went to in the resurrection. All four gospels place her at the tomb at the resurrection of Jesus. This is almost the one piece of information in which all four gospels are consistent. Jesus chooses wisely. He knows, He trusts, He believes in the women. In the women He is sure the New Covenant will not be abandoned.

"Mary Magdalene came, and announced to the disciples, 'I have seen the Lord, and these things He has said to me" (see John 20:1-18). She was told by Jesus to go and "evangelize," to announce the good news. Mary Magdalene was the first to continue the work of salvation. She was filled with the power of the Holy Spirit.

Pentecost

In the Holy Bible, in Acts, the author Luke tells us "During the forty days after Jesus' crucifixion, He appeared to the apostles from time to time. In one of those meetings, He told the apostles not to leave Jerusalem until the Holy Spirit came upon them." Jesus said to them, "You shall be baptized with the Holy Spirit in just a few days." Jesus also said to His apostles, "When the Holy Spirit has come upon you, you will receive power to testify about me with great effect." (see Acts 1:3-8)

The men, the apostles, the 12, the reason for a male headship, had not even yet received the Holy Spirit. The women were already filled with the Holy Spirit. The women were about 33 years ahead of the guys.

At the Birth Announcement, also called the Annunciation, the angel said to Mary of Nazareth, "The Holy Spirit will come upon you and the power of the Most High will overshadow you." Mary's response: a resounding "Yes!" "Let it be according to your word."

Mary of Nazareth was now the "temple of the Holy Spirit," God's new covenant. Mary was one with the Holy Spirit; Mary was now spouse of the Holy Spirit, Mother of Jesus, and therefore the mother of God according to Christian teaching. So I ask you, where is the male headship?

When Elizabeth heard Mary's greeting, "Elizabeth was filled with the Holy Spirit."

It was Mary Magdalene Jesus went to first in the resurrection. She was the first witness, she was told by Jesus to go and evangelize, go and tell my brethren.

It was these women who were filled with the Holy Spirit long before the 12 apostles. These women were the first witnesses to this man Jesus Christ. Mary of Nazareth and "several other women" had to be present at "Pentecost" (see Acts 1:14). I am sure Mary Magdalene was present – it would be silly to argue she was not there. By Mary of Nazareth's presence, the gift of the Holy Spirit was showered on the 12 apostles and all disciples of faith. Mary is one with the Holy Spirit; she is God's spouse; "And the two shall become one."

We will never be true to God's new covenant until we acknowledge that the formal agreement – the contract – was carried out by courageous Jewish women demanding a just and peaceful world for all the children of God.

Last, but not least, we must empower women and motherhood through faith and courage, learning what God already knows: Our mothers are the most sacred beings next only to God.

A Personal Note

In this section I speak with full confidence that Mary of Nazareth has been my spiritual guide for as long as I can remember. But only recently have I stopped and truly communicated with this extraordinarily courageous woman. She is with me every day. Mary will never let me rest until this little book is complete.

Although I am college educated, I have no advanced degrees. I am not sophisticated, intellectual, or scholarly. I am not religious: I feel empty at church. And yet I love Jesus and His mother, Mary, beyond words. More and more, I feel their presence within me. My eyes have been opened by their example and message. And although I still have human bouts of anger, sadness, and regrets of my sins – especially hurting other people with impatience, words, and actions, be that my husband, children, or complete strangers, I still know I am loved. I am aware I must improve my soul and be good to all people. I fail daily, but I refuse to give up. I believe my mission and your mission, is simply to put our feet on the floor each morning and with the help of God someplace deep within every soul, try and face the trivial, the mundane, and the routine with courage, knowing that each being you come in contact with is also depending on you in some way to acknowledge their worth, their presence, their dreams and their fears, for all of us are restlessly seeking God. Listen. Listen to yourself, your children, your spouse, your partner, your friends, but greatest of all, listen to the stranger. To listen is to care, to believe, to affirm one's worth.

PAUL! PAUL! PAUL! WHAT HAVE YOU DONE?

The Catholic church, and Christianity today in general, is more St. Paul-like than Christ-like because it takes its teachings from the repressed soul of Paul instead of the inclusive life lessons of Jesus.

> Paul took leadership and authority away from women. Not so Jesus. (I Timothy 2:11-12)
>
> Paul forbade women to speak in the church. Not so Jesus. (I Corinthians 14:34)
>
> Paul made husbands head of their wives. Not so Jesus. (Ephesians 5:23)
>
> Paul told women to be submissive. Not so Jesus. (I Corinthians 14:34-35)
>
> Paul said a woman's salvation is by way of pain of child bearing. Not so Jesus. (I Timothy 2:15)
>
> Paul had a problem with sex. Not so Jesus.
>
> Paul had a problem with the human body. Not so Jesus. (Romans 6:12-13, 7:15-24)

Paul said celibacy is more holy than two spirits coming together in mutual love and respect. Not so Jesus. (I Corinthians 7:7-9, 32-34)

Paul told women to cover their heads. Not so Jesus. (I Corinthians 11:5-6)

Paul said all people are sinners and fall short of God's glory. Not so Jesus.

Paul went back to the old ways of power, control, and intolerance. Not so Jesus.

Paul claimed his authority was the "word of the lord". No. Never. Not once did Jesus say women were to be silent in the church. Not once did Jesus say women have no authority over men. His mother was His authority figure. He was flesh of her flesh. Jesus was part of her faith, wisdom, and courage.

Remember that the most astounding and revolutionary change Jesus brought to first century Judaism was His full inclusion of women at God's altar and the table of life. Yes, women were Jesus' friends, peers, companions, confidants, disciples, and, yes, apostles.

This Paul was way out of line when he spoke about and against women. Paul did not like women; He denigrated them. Jesus loved women; He respected them. Paul hated the human body; he felt the human body was evil, especially two spirits coming together. Jesus loved the human body. He liked getting close to people, touching people. I am sure Jesus and Mary Magdalene shared a bed as husband and wife. She was always with Him. Remember, she was the only person looking or trying to claim His body after the crucifixion.

Perhaps the most un-Christ-like thing Paul did was to exclude women at God's altar and place celibacy above two spirits coming together in mutual love and respect. Celibacy does not make you closer to God. Celibacy does not make you more holy.

How could Paul tell us "There is neither Jew nor Greek, there is neither male and female, for you are all one in Christ Jesus," and then hang out a sign "men only", women need not apply? What happened? Why did Paul abandon women? Jesus never did.

Jesus said to Martha, "There is really only one thing worth being concerned about, Mary has discovered it, and I will not take it away from her." Paul did exactly what Jesus would not do. He sent the women back into the kitchen to serve only by tending to their husbands' needs. She can't serve God and her husband. He would take care of God, she will take care of her husband. Paul said, "I permit no women to teach or have authority over men." Paul took the easy way out: the safe popular route. The men were complaining the women weren't home and dinner was late. The women were out front and center teaching the good news. The women were preaching the good news of equality and acceptance: the only way to peace and salvation for all of God's children. So Paul gave in to the pressure of the men. He did not want to lose his newfound power, control, and position here on earth. Not so Jesus.

The exclusion of women by St. Paul and later by the bishops in the early days of Christianity amounts to nothing short of the ruthless destruction of the true Christ movement. The men perhaps left the periphery of Christianity but they destroyed the true center.

MODERN DAY ST. PAULS: THE PROSECUTING ATTORNEYS OF OUR CHILDREN'S SOULS

A Brief Review

Remember, the degradation of women and human sexuality in the Christian movement began with St. Paul. Then the first bishops of The Church carried on the "no women need apply" attitude. Sexism and a negative view of the human body and sexuality in general gathered momentum with the unnatural thinking of celibate men. Here are a few of these men:

> **St. Augustine:** Augustine believed for men to grow spiritually they must avoid women. He also believed men must control women's place in society. St. Augustine insisted the virgin birth was a must in order to protect Jesus' divinity[5].

---

[5] *In Search of Mary* by Sally Cunneen, pp.111-122

St. Jerome: Jerome preached that sex is the "vomit of marriage." Jerome also said pregnant women are a "revolting spectacle."

St. Ambrose: Ambrose went around recruiting rich virgins to join The Church so The Church could profit from their wealth, and in return, they could be free of a husband and childbearing. However in the fourth century, this was actually a good deal for women. This doesn't say much for traditional values.

What Christian Groups in America Today Teach Our Children

Evangelical Protestants are the most common religious group in America today (26%). Mainline Protestants are 17%. Catholics are 23%, the largest single Christian church with a hierarchy and the second largest religion in the world[6].

This means that at least 50% of Christians in America are taught that theirs is a male headship and women are

---

[6] "Religion" by David van Biena, *Time Magazine*, May 13, 1996

inferior to men. This does not even count all the other religions in America that teach women are inferior, such as orthodox Jews, Muslims, and Mormons.

All of these religions mentioned also teach that homosexuality (a natural process) is evil.

For these religions to teach our children that women are inferior and homosexuality is evil is plain wrong. This follows St. Paul, not Jesus Christ. In this section I speak as a woman with 50 years of Roman Catholic experience.

A Modern Day St. Paul: Pope John Paul II

(The Papal quotes and conversations with Undersecretary of The United Nations' Conference on Population and Development, Nafis Sadik, were taken from Carl Bernstein and Marco Politi's Book, *His Holiness*, pp.519-524.)

Don't you think that the irresponsible behavior of men is caused by women. spoken in the spring of 1994 by Pope John Paul II. So much for "feminine genius" written by the Pope in an apostolic letter titled, "The Dignity of Women."

There is no dignity, respect, freedom, or justice for women in the Roman Catholic Church when its leader,

Pope John Paul II, makes it clear that he thinks women are responsible for all the world's problems. His unChrist-like behavior toward women is slowly dividing The Church to a degree from which it may not recover.

Pope John Paul II: the man who could free Poland but refuses democratic rights for almost one billion Catholics worldwide. In my eyes, and I believe in the eyes of God, his two biggest failures as Pope are his cold stand on birth control, choice, and his refusal to do as Jesus Christ did: open the door to women to stand equal to men at God's altar. After all, Mary of Nazareth was the first apostle. She was the founder of the new faith movement. Peter abandoned and denied Jesus. Mary Magdalene, not a man, was the first to hear and evangelize the "good news". Pope John Paul II is an educated man; he must realize there was no male headship instituted by Jesus. Yes, women can and must be allowed to serve The Church as priests.

Pope John Paul's View on Birth Control

The Pope says "family planning can be practiced only in accordance with moral, spiritual, and natural laws." Now I ask Pope John Paul II what is more unnatural than himself, his cardinals, bishops, and priests being celibate and excluding women from God's altar?

Again, celibacy is not natural or normal. Celibacy does not bring you closer to God, nor does it make you holy. If one chooses to be celibate, that should be respected. On the other hand, if one chooses to share the gift of human sexuality with a person he or she loves and cares for, that should be respected as well.

Natural birth control is unreliable and women suffer the consequences. When women suffer consequences, their children also suffer, sons and daughters equally. Take it from me – natural birth control does not work. At the age of 32 I was married ten years and had five children. I was not open to procreating anymore. I was physically, mentally, and spiritually suffering the consequences of having too many children, not to mention the economic stress it put on my my relationship and marriage with my husband.

Finally, I chose to have my tubes tied. God cheered me on and completely respected my choice as sane and wise. Now my church, the Roman Catholic Church, says I am not following Church teaching because I chose to have my tubes tied. Because I am not following Church teaching, I am not supposed to receive Holy Communion at Mass. I have a news flash for all priests, bishops, cardinals, and the Pope: almost every Catholic woman from age 18 to 50+ uses some form of "unnatural" birth control. Does this make it right? Does this make it moral? You're darn right it does! Because it is about the well being of a woman's body, mind, and soul, and that of the children she chooses to have.

I always believed if Pope John Paul II was forced to baby-sit my five children for one week with no help, no cooks, no secretaries, no maids, or housekeeping, he would have started his own birth control company. John Paul II must also remember this: having five children was tough on me physically, mentally, and economically, yet I had a supportive husband. We are both educated (registered nurses) and we had a home and regular income. John Paul II has to think about all the women who live with little support and no education and women in developing countries who live in shacks with dirt floors. This does not make them holy or close to God. It makes the women feel hopelessness and despair. The children these women already have suffer more as they see their mothers growing wearier.

The Pope and Choice

I believe, especially in developing countries, to deny access to contraceptives is to promote abortion. No woman should be forced to carry, grow, and nourish a child in her womb for nine months if she does not want to. Every woman has a right to say to God, "No, I am sorry, but I am weary and I can't physically or mentally carry this child now. My other children need me, my body and mind can not take any more." God understands this, women. No male religious leader or male legislator has any business dictating what is a woman's choice. This is not a person outside a woman's body on life support (the child in the womb); this is a child inside a woman's body, affecting her body, mind, soul, and well-being. A woman has a right to say "yes" or "no," free consent.

Remember, delivering a baby is always life threatening to the mother's health; there is always a risk factor. Should male religious and legislative leaders force her to undergo this stress and risk? Is the woman's life not sacred? Does she not deserve the sanctity of her life?

To force a woman to carry a child is putting the woman's life at great risk. Because, when forced, her physical and mental state will be severely compromised.

Pope John Paul II knows that the highest rate of illegal abortion is in poorer catholic countries. How can this educated man deny these suffering women birth control? Because of his naive, cold, ridiculous view of women and suffering, Pope John Paul II continues to personally crush the souls of many children with the ongoing oppression of their mothers. A woman's life must be considered sacred.

"There are no individual rights and needs. There can be only the couples' rights and needs," spoken by Pope John Paul II in the spring of 1994. The woman who was present when the pope made this remark quickly shot back, "Women are the ones who get pregnant and in many societies women don't have equal status with men." Pope John Paul II did not like this woman who told him the truth about women and pregnancy. Her name was Nafis Sadik, Undersecretary of the United Nation's Conference on Population and Development. She told the pope it is children and mothers who suffer the consequences of oversized families. Sadik continued, "Many women, you know, wind up abandoned. Latin America is full of abandoned families full of women who are left as heads of the households, with children to look after, while the men go off and start another family somewhere else."

On the subject of birth control, Sadik asked Pope John Paul II, "How many Catholics do you think actually follow the teachings of The Church on this matter?"

The pope responded, "It is only the Catholics in those materialistic developed societies who don't. All the people in the poorer countries do."

Sadik said to Pope John Paul II, "I am sorry to have to disagree with you, because in Latin America, for example, women have no access to contraceptives," Sadik noted, "and so they resort to abortion. In fact, we find the highest rate of illegal abortion in many of the poorer catholic countries in the world."

Her meeting with Pope John Paul II was now over. "Sadik walked out on to St. Peter's Square feeling disappointed by the lack of compassion in the man." "He doesn't like women," she commented later. "I expected a little more sympathy for suffering and death."

About a week after Pope John Paul II's visit with this woman, Nafis Sadik, the Pope declared war against American feminism, western societies, and the United

Nations for their view on birth control, choice, and empowering women with individual rights[7]. Pope John Paul II and his Vatican diplomats set out to seek an alliance with Islam. They began "courting the most fundamentalist and extremist Islamic countries" including Libya and Iran. Pope John Paul II was determined to control women and reproduction.

The Roman Catholic Church, my church, cries loudly in reference to social justice, especially compassion for the poor and the unborn. Justice, freedom and human dignity, John Paul II, often evokes such words and thoughts. The truth is, The Church has no rights when it comes to social justice and the family. Mother Church is weeping daily for its sins against our mothers, sisters, and daughters, and our homosexual brothers and sisters.

The disintegration of the family and the culture of death is not caused by American feminism, western societies, or gays and lesbians as Pope John Paul II, among other conservative fundamentalist religious leaders, likes to frequently suggest. The disintegration of the family and the culture of death are the Roman Catholic Church's teachings and all religions who teach the continued outright

---

[7] *His Holiness* by Carl Bernstein and Marco Politi, pp.524-525

oppression of women and our gay and lesbian brothers and sisters. Traditional families always included strong women with free consent and always included gay and lesbian members. Unless a cultural change pierces the heart and soul of The Church, hopelessness and despair will continue to creep into our souls.

Pope John Paul II is cold, unrelenting, and unChrist-like when it comes to women. He insists women submit to the teachings of the pope and the bishop even at the cost of a mother's life and those of her children. Pope John Paul II must remember that when you abandon the mother, a woman, you abandon her children, sons and daughters equally. This is the greatest violence against all humanity.

Pope John Paul II and the catholic hierarchy practice *un*-christ-like behavior by excluding women, divorced people, married priests, and gay and lesbian people and even people using artificial birth control. All of these groups of people are part of God's family and are part of traditional families. The Church is destroying the family, not feminists. In fact, feminists, or strong, educated women, are and will be the salvation of the family. Justice, freedom, and democracy are feminist values, not Church values.

It is The Church that teaches our sons and daughters that God discriminates against their mother, that God made women second class citizens. It is The Church that teaches our children that to be closer to God – to be more holy – you should not have sex, you should live alone, be a nun or a priest; Being celibate is is the best way to serve God. This is the most unnatural state, totally against natural law, that you could teach our children. It is The Church that teaches our children that marriage is the second best way to serve God and have sex only when you are open to procreate. Yet we women, mothers, continue to fill the pews every Sunday with our children and listen to the men on the altar wearing their elegant robes. These men have become princes of The Church instead of servants to the people as Jesus taught them ("Do as I have done to you.") And we let these men continue to be the prosecuting attorneys of our children's souls.

The Pope's Battleground

Women's birth control, women's choice, and women's ordination: The three big NO's. If this is Pope John Paul II's idea of the dignity of women, then I suggest he needs a refresher course in the New Testament 101.

Christ chose only men as his Apostles. Written by Pope John Paul II in his 1994 papal document, "Priestly Ordination." Of course anybody who reads the New Testament knows this is not true. God chose a woman, not a man. The word "apostle" is defined as a leader or a teacher of a new faith movement. It was Mary of Nazareth who became one with the Holy Spirit, one with God. She was Jesus' teacher and authority figure. Jesus was flesh of her flesh. The twelve Apostles were anemic in faith, weak kneed cowards who abandoned, denounced, betrayed, and doubted Jesus Christ. Now somebody, anybody, tell me where is the male headship? Why do women continue to accept this false teaching by most Christian churches? The outright oppression of women is deeply rooted in this theology. How can our children, our sons and daughters, ever believe in equality or have respect for each other or themselves if Pope John Paul II and every other religious fundamentalist continue to teach them "Christ chose only men as his Apostles." This perhaps is the greatest lie ever told about who Jesus Christ was and what he stood for. Perhaps the greatest sin is educated women who continue to accept this teaching, because it continues to shackle the souls of our children, sons and daughters equally.

We Shall Overcome

"Over the years, with rare exceptions, women had been the only ones to contradict John Paul II in front of large audiences." How ironic for the legacy of Pope John Paul II it will be women, feminism that will be the salvation of our children's souls. Yes, feminists will insist on a true democracy with real social justice and freedom for the world's sons and daughters, not the pope.

Pope John Paul II spoke eloquently in reference to the communist regime in China. The pope said, "Millions of believers can't be constantly oppressed, placed under suspicion, and kept divided." Pope John Paul II should heed his own words when it comes to women and their place at God's altar. John Paul's teachings continue to oppress and divide nations, communities, and worst of all, families. This is the root of all human suffering.

Our Gay and Lesbian Sons and Daughters

Pope John Paul II and The Church's hierarchy not only continue to brutalize the souls of women, but also the souls of our gay and lesbian sons and daughters. Women and homosexuals have this in common: we are refused a place at God's altar and, therefore, the table of life. Women and homosexuals are not fully accepted by our churches and therefore we are not accepted by our communities and our families as full and equal members.

"A family is a husband, a wife, and their children. And marriage is the only basis for a family. Homosexuals and lesbians are not families," spoken by Pope John Paul II at the Vatican in 1994. All I can say to this is "may God forgive them." By "them" I mean all the world's religious hierarchy that teach exclusion, hate, pain, suffering, and bring anguish to mothers, fathers, sisters, brothers, grandmothers and grandfathers by teaching traditional (or normal) families should be ashamed if their son or daughter is gay or lesbian.

The 1998 version of a national conference of catholic bishops, a pastoral message to parents of gays and lesbians titled, *Always Our Children* sold out to the demands of Pope John Paul II and The Church hierarchy. The 1997 version of *Always Our Children* had a more wholesome, truthful, and Christ-like message. It noted that a homosexual orientation was not considered sinful. The 1998 version added: Homosexuality is "objectively disordered." How St. Paul-like could they get? They sell out the people's souls to retain their own earthly power and position.

TRADITIONAL FAMILIES: Traditional families are, and have always included our gay and lesbian sons and daughters. It is not the role of religion to change a natural process. I have no doubt that homosexuality is part of God's divine plan. Human sexuality is part of who we are. It is one of the great spiritual gifts from God. Human sexuality is natural and good, and not just for procreation. When God said, "Be fruitful and multiply" I suppose it was a great plan – a great idea. Since there were only two people, one male, one female, it made sense at the time. Perhaps, as the Catholic Church believes, they should have chosen celibacy to be pure and love God best.

Two spirits coming together, be it woman to woman, man to man, or woman to man, is spiritual, natural, and good when done with mutual love, respect, and commitment. Remember, celibacy is not natural or normal. Celibacy does not bring you close to God. The Church is the most unnatural family. They exclude women and they exclude sex that is not open to procreation. Yet they demand that women use only natural birth control and only have sex if they are married.

So, let's sum it up. The only members of the Roman Catholic Church considered faithful are:

1) Mom and Dad in a committed marriage who have sex only if they are open to procreate – and neither can have been divorced.

2) Their children, Dick and Jane, who must be heterosexual and celibate until marriage.

3) A nun or a priest who never thinks about sex.

Yes, according to the teachings of Pope John Paul II and the Catholic hierarchy, only these people are the faithful and worthy to receive Christ at holy communion during mass.

The New Millennium

Pope John Paul II wrote in his apostolic letter titled *As the Third Millennium Approaches*: "'The time has come to repent,' the pope proclaimed, 'every Christian should adhere to the wise words of the second Vatican council. Truth cannot be imposed except by the force of the truth itself.'"

The truth is, it is time for the Roman Catholic Church and all the Christian churches as well as Muslim and Jewish religious leaders alike to apologize to our mothers, sisters, and daughters and our gay and lesbian brothers and sisters. It is time to apologize to them for perpetuating the two accepted forms of intolerance, hate, and even violence, these being sexism and homophobia.

Society believes it is okay for religions to teach discrimination against women and homosexuals because, after all, God discriminates against them.

Rome, December 25, 1999
The first day of the holy year 2000
Pope John Paul II Speaks: Respect, Tolerance, and Repentance
(Papal quotes from a story written by Alessandra Stanley for the Seattle Post-Intelligencer, Dec. 1999)

John Paul II said, "At times people have refused to respect and love their brothers of a different faith or race. They have denied fundamental rights to individuals and nations."

How true, but this will always be so until we admit the root of this continued prejudice, bigotry, and discrimination. This root is the church hierarchy's refusal to respect and love our mothers, daughters, and sisters simply because of their gender. The Church continues to deny fundamental rights to our mothers and therefore continues to crush the soul of every family, community, and nation.

The Pope also said, "Christ, you are the door. Through you, in the power of the Holy Spirit, we wish to enter the third millennium."

"The power of the Holy Spirit" is his mother, Mary of Nazareth. She became one with the Holy Spirit. Therefore, she is the Holy Spirit. Mary is God's new covenant. Mary is the founder of a new faith movement. Mary molded and nourished the soul of Jesus. He was flesh of her flesh. Mary of Nazareth and her seed, Jesus, would change the unjust ways of men.

I agree with Pope John Paul II, we all wish to enter the third millennium but not without our mothers, sisters, and daughters fully equal to our fathers, brothers, and sons at God's altar. Then, and only then, will we be equal at the table of life.

When the church hierarchy stops teaching our sons and daughters that women are incomplete or inferior human beings, that women need not apply, that women are sent to the back of the bus, then the church can claim a fullness of Christian morality. The same holds true for church teachings regarding our non-celibate gay and lesbian sons and daughters.

Just Words

Yes, no matter how you word it ("Always Our Children," "Dignity of Women," "The Genius of Women," or "We love you, but not your sin"), the truth is The Church is still teaching sexism and homophobia to our sons and daughters. Freedom of religion should not include the right to teach intolerance because hate and violence in the name of God are the end result. Any and all religions who teach a male headship or profess homosexual love is evil must stop. Churches are inflicting severe suffering on the souls of every family because every family includes women and every family has a gay, lesbian, or bisexual member -and that is the plain truth of traditional families.

I don't believe the church leaders will bring about this change. I do believe each person must demand the churches accept change by simply insisting that men and women are equal at God's altar and therefore the table of life. And that two consenting adults who have a mutual sexual attraction with the needed ingredients of love and respect, be it man to man, woman to woman, or woman to man, two spirits coming together is always natural and good.

Consistent Prejudice

Yes, Pope John Paul II and The Church hierarchy have been clear and unmistakable in its unjust prejudice against women, our mothers, our sons and daughters and homosexuals. One must remember that in all four gospels Jesus never mentioned homosexuality as a sin and God's New Covenant began with a woman, not a man. She and her seed would change the ways of men.

Religion, in whatever form, Christian, Jewish, or Islamic, must stop being used as a tool to oppress and instead start liberating the souls of our children. The Church must be aware sexism breeds sexist acts. Religions must never instill guilt or fear, only love and acceptance.

Other Modern Day Pauls

Other well known religious and political men who embrace the teachings of the repressed soul St. Paul, instead of the inclusive life lessons of Jesus are: Pat Robertson, Jerry Falwell, Gary Bauer, Ralph Reed, Alan

Keys, Bill Bennett, Patrick Buchanan, James Dobson, and Reggie White. Like Pope John Paul II, they think women should sit at the back of the bus and our gay and lesbian sons and daughters are evil.

These self-righteous men use power, control and fear techniques to keep the faithful in their proper place. Sounds to me a lot like St. Paul, not Jesus Christ.

THE WORD GAME

Both political and religious conservatives successfully make people believe God is on their side by using key words over and over again. When I turn on the television, listen to the radio, or read news stories I see, hear, or read about these same men all the time. They seem angry; they are full of righteous indignation. Who are these men? They are the same bunch from the previous section of this book. Pat Robertson, Jerry Falwell, James Dobson, Ralph Reed, Pope John Paul II, Gary Bauer, Alan Keys, Bill Bennett, Patrick Buchanan, and a newcomer, the retired linebacker Rev. Reggie White.

I guess we could say these men are eloquent. They speak fluently and powerfully. Some people might be confused and consider these men noble. I am sure they think of themselves as noble. Noble is to possess excellent qualities, especially in one's character, free from pettiness or meanness. Three subjects come to mind that these men are obsessed with:

1) Their arrogance or exaggerated feeling of their superiority when it comes to matters that involve our mothers, sisters, and daughters. They would insist, demand, or make a woman carry a child in her womb for nine months even if she physically or mentally felt she could not carry the child to term. When it comes to contraception, some of these men say a firm, "No." And when it comes to women being equal at God's altar, these men still believe and teach our children that God thinks their mothers are inferior.
2) Their total vilification of our precious gay and lesbian sons and daughters. One day soon they will have to stand up and apologize to the world for their hate and intolerance of a natural process.
3) Their petty and mean-spirited behavior towards our president, Bill Clinton, a man with more character than all of these men put together.

The Words They Use:

Sacred or Sanctity - Two beautiful words often invoked by these men when speaking about a woman's right to abortion or to choice. Sacred and sanctity are very close in meaning, that is: associated with or dedicated to God or regarded with reverence.

Holiness, sacredness. When I think of these words I think of my mother, motherhood, or a mother struggling, sacrificing to care, love, nurture, and teach the children she has already brought into this world. Her children are sacred and need their mother to be healthy, strong, wise, and loving. I ask, is she not sacred also, is she not holy and to be regarded with reverence? God thinks so. God will respect her choice to give birth to her child or give the soul back to God because she is physically, mentally, and economically unable to carry the child to term. These men have no right to use these beautiful words because it is their very teachings that deny women basic democratic rights within their own religion. They have all but erased the sacredness of women, our own mothers.

Culture of Death - These guys are the culture of death. They could all carry little black bags around with an inscription, "Dr. Death. We kill women." Here's the formula:

1) God thinks women are inferior; they are not as holy or good as men.
2) God is sexist, so it is okay to be sexist.
3) You will carry that baby to term. We don't care about your body or health. You must give your life and deliver this child -and we don't care about the five other children you leave behind.
4) No contraceptives, but submit to your husbands.

Bible Morality - How often do we hear this expression? We must get back to a tradition of biblical morality. If Gary Bauer, Jerry Falwell, Pat Robertson, and Alan Keyes spouted this once, they spouted it a hundred times. I chuckle every time I hear it. This is how I know very few people really read the bible because so-called biblical morality is not what I want my sons and daughters to emulate. There are exceptions of course in both the Old and New Testaments; the most prominent to me is Mary of Nazareth, her son Jesus, and Mary Magdalene who truly were one with the Holy Spirit. I would want my sons and daughters to emulate their courage, love, determination, and faith. However, most biblical morality is not something to aspire to.

Biblical: means Jewish or Christian scriptures, Old or New Testament.

Morality: means moral principles, goodness or rightness.

Do we want to go back to a moral principle that upheld that:

1) Women were men's property; they had little or no rights.
2) Slavery was acceptable.
3) Male children are far more superior to female children.
4) Most biblical leaders with the exception of Jesus (but including St. Paul) ruled with fear, guilt, power control, and most of all judgment. Instead of presenting God as a loving father and mother, they portrayed a vengeful, jealous God.

To biblical morality I say a firm, "No." I will not bring my children or grandchildren back to the days of acceptable racism, sexism, ethnic cleansing, and homophobia.

Virtue - Here is Bill Bennett's favorite word. He even wrote a book called The Book of Virtues. Virtue means: moral excellence, goodness, or chastity. As I read the bible, I find few people who are virtuous and when I do run across them, they are almost always women or women who raised virtuous sons as Mary and Elizabeth did.

Does Bill Bennett think he is of moral excellence? Every time I hear him speak he sounds petty, mean-spirited, and judgmental. I ask, is this a virtuous man?

Character - Every political person's new favorite word. Character means: *all* those qualities that make a person different from others. A person's moral nature, a person's moral strength.

Most conservatives say President Bill Clinton is a man of poor character. Hogwash! Bill Clinton is a man of good character. He cares and fights for people of color, women's rights, gay rights, and has taught our children ethnic cleansing is wrong. I can't say the same for the character of the group of men listed in this section. Many of us have character flaws, but at the same time we have character strengths. I think President Clinton's strengths are great. And I think the character flaws of Gary Bauer, Alan Keyes,

Pat Buchanan, Jerry Falwell, Bill Bennett, and James Dobson are many. Their characters seem to be the very thing Jesus preached against, that is: judgment, control, revenge, intolerance, and hate.

Inviolable - Not to be violated. Pope John Paul II and the Catholic hierarchy use this word frequently on the subject of abortion or pro-choice women. This is a strong word "not to be violated." To this, what must be said is that first, the Catholic hierarchy must stop violating a woman's basic God-given democratic rights. That is, to be full and equal members at God's altar and the table of life. Second, the Catholic hierarchy must stop violating a woman's basic God-given right to choose. "Her choice" on how many children she is able to grow in her body and how many children she is able to nourish and love in her life. This is up to her and her God only. It is not up to a group of old celibate men to tell a woman, a mother, how to live. The unnatural thinking of these celibate men is perhaps one of the greatest violations against humanity.

Pro-Family - Don't be fooled when ultra conservatives use this word; they are not pro-family. All families have mothers, sisters, and daughters and these guys continue to deny them full equality at God's altar and the table of life. Many families have gay and lesbian children and these guys continue to crucify their very souls.

Feminist - A supporter (man or woman) of women's claims to be given rights, opportunities, and treatment equal to those of men.

Pope John Paul II, Pat Robertson, Jerry Falwell, Gary Bauer, James Dobson, Alan Keyes, Bill Bennett, Patrick Buchanan, Ralph Reed, and Reggie White use the word "feminist" as if it were shameful and dirty. Well hang on to your hats, boys, because it is the feminists who will ensure a true democracy with social justice and freedom for our sons and daughters. It is the religious right who ensure democratic rights to men only. Oh, I mean "straight men only. Women and homosexuals need not apply."

The word game has worked well for the ultra conservatives, the Christian right and Catholic hierarchy, because we as a society, we as a people, and we as a nation believed our feminist mothers and sisters, and our gay and lesbian sons and daughters had no place in a pro-family or traditional family conversation. Yet we the people are getting smarter, soon the word game won't work because what we are coming to realize is traditional families and pro-family values include *all* members of our family, not just a few.

SELECTIVE SIN

Selective - Chosen or choosing carefully.

Sin - Breaking of a religious or moral law, an act that does this.

Almost all major religions are guilty of selective sin from the holy bible. Some examples of what used to be considered sinful, defiled or possessed of Satan are: being left-handed, sleeping or even touching a menstruating woman, having epilepsy, touching a dead person or animal, a pimple, boil, or birthmark on the face. There are so many more examples, just read Leviticus for starters.

Today we would be embarrassed to label anyone of these a sin, defiled or possessed of Satan. However religions continue to latch on to "a man lying with a man is an abomination" and "women have no authority in The Church." This is selective sin, and it is simply wrong and should not be tolerated.

Sodom and Gomorrah - Whenever most people hear this bible story mentioned they think, "homosexuality," which shows that most bible thumpers are poor students of scripture. Sodom and Gomorrah were wicked places alright, but they had nothing to do with homosexuality and everything to do with violence, rape, hate, intolerance, and sexism.

"They had not so much as lain down when the townspeople, the men of Sodom, young and old from every quarter began to close in upon the house, clamoring to Lot. 'Where are those men who came to you this evening? Bring them out to us. We want to get close to them.' Lot went out to this mob, shutting the door behind him. 'Please, brothers,' he begged, 'don't be wicked. Listen, I have two daughters who have never been with a man. Let me bring them out to you and you can do what you like to them. Only do nothing bad to these men" (Gen. 19:4-9).

First of all, do I believe all the men, young and old alike are gay? I don't think so. Even if that were the case it is not a story of homosexual love but one of force, abuse, violence, and rape. This is not a story of two mature consenting adults. Perhaps greatest of all, this story is about women being considered sub-human and the property of a man. The women have little or no value.

Nobody ever questions the good and righteous Lot and his decision to throw his virgin daughters to a violent mob of men and "do what you like with them." This story should be revisited and studied by feminist groups and gay advocates so people like Pat Robertson and Jerry Falwell can be told they are biblically ignorant if they believe that the story of Sodom and Gomorrah speaks against homosexuality. However, it speaks volumes for biblical morality and the status of women. It speaks volumes about the "wickedness" of rape, violence, intolerance, and social injustice practiced by the men of Sodom including Lot. This man, a father, would throw his virgin daughters out to be raped and brutalized by a mob of vicious men. Was this the righteous man God wanted to save?

Now Lot left Sodom and went to the hills where he lived with his two daughters in a cave. One day the daughters decided to get father drunk and have sex with him. "Come, let us ply our father with wine, then sleep with him and so make life with our father's seed" (Gen. 19:32). All the years I went to church, had religion in school every morning, and went to Sunday school, I never remember going over the complete story of Sodom and Gomorrah. Now I know why. I wonder if Jerry Falwell and Pat Robertson think this is a traditional family, or is this the biblical morality they speak of?

St. Paul - According to many Christians, the other reason for believing homosexuality is not natural or is evil is because of our good friend the repressed soul St. Paul. He talks about homosexuality in Corinthians and Romans. Can Paul be taken seriously here; does he have any credibility? After all, Paul also said the following:

1) Man only is the image and glory of God.
2) Paul prohibited a woman from speaking in the church saying she was a subordinate creature. She is not fully human. (I Corinthians 11:7-9)
3) Paul also blamed women for man's sin and said the only way to be saved is through bearing children. (I guess all those Catholic nuns including the holy Mother Theresa are not saved.)
4) He permitted no women to teach or have authority over men. (I guess this is news to most good mothers and wives, for most are the authority and teachers in their families.)
5) Paul also said the husband is head of his wife.

Saint Paul's thinking was unlike Christ's regarding the full inclusion and equality of women and he seemed to not like sex in general. He certainly never thought of human sexuality as a spiritual gift from God. Why should we believe he is right about homosexuality? I don't even think he understood today's definition of homosexuality. Don't forget, at his time in history, they did not understand a menstruating woman. Nobody was allowed near her. The bible says: "Whoever touches her shall be unclean" (Leviticus 15:19; also see Leviticus 20:18).

Paul also believed and taught "obey the government for God is the one who put it there" (Romans 13:1). Does this mean we don't challenge government when it is wrong or unjust? Of course not. St. Paul, like all of us, had a few demons to deal with. Paul's view on homosexuality holds no water when it comes to the love of two mature loving adults sharing their life together. It is natural for people of the same gender to have a relationship. There is nothing unnatural about two mature people wanting to love and share their lives, including a bed. This is natural and good as long as you love and respect one another. It is not about sexual anatomy; it's about hearts and souls and sharing in the spirit of God.

The inerrant word of God - Inerrant means not liable to error. Every word in the bible is to be taken literally? Sorry, I don't buy this because if St. Paul is right about his views on women, human sexuality, slaves, Jews, and government, then God is not a just God nor is God a very nice being. However, I know the spirit of God is not this way and Paul is just plain wrong. If religious leaders like Pat Robertson, Jerry Falwell, Gary Bauer, and Reggie White really believe that the bible is inerrant, then they are truly biblically ignorant.

One of the best examples that most Christians would be familiar with is the birth narrative. The gospels of Luke and Matthew differ greatly on many details. Which gospel is true? Which gospel is the inerrant word of God? The only reason to teach that the bible is the inerrant word of God is to keep the people in the pews controlled, fearful, and have authority over their very souls.

Yes, religions have chosen to be selective about which sins are the greatest and which sins to keep on the books. The two they have selected are homosexuality and feminism. The religious right goes into convulsions when they hear these two words. To me, the words bring good thoughts, even noble thoughts like social justice, freedom, democracy, partners, equality, and sharing.

GIRLS CAN'T…

Even in the Movies - During the making of the movie *The Prince of Egypt*, an expert in interfaith relationships was hired as liaison to the religious community. The producers and directors were very careful as not to offend any race, creed, or color. However, when it came to gender, nobody worried about offending women. All those evangelists and rabbis who were consultants on the film made sure women were kept in their place. What is even worse, Dream Works let it happen.

"The voice of God was one of the more difficult choices in the film. Every race and color and creed has a claim to the voice of God," Katzenberg says. Using an idea of producer Cox's, the animators put together a scratch track that was an eerily effective chorus of every character in the film, with the dominate voice morphing from man to woman, to child. But consultant Schwartz-Getzug vetoed that approach, saying, "some people would be offended if the voice of God sounded, even momentarily, like a woman's." (Written by Kim Masters for *Time Magazine*, December 14, 1998.)

If, instead of women, the above statement had made reference to any race, creed, or color, it would have been absolutely unacceptable, especially in reference to God. Yet, nobody blinked an eye when it came to degrading the status of women and their relationship to God and religion. Why? Because the outright second-class status of women has been legitimized by almost every major religion – not by God, but by men and their interpretations of God. This is truly the root of every other prejudice, every other oppression in human history.

A Mother's Story - Another example of "Girls can't…" is told beautifully by author Blu Greenberg in her book, *On Women and Judaism*: "On the last Sabbath that my husband served as rabbi of a congregation, the children and I decided to surprise him. Moshe, then ten, prepared the haftarah reading, David, nine, the An' im Zemirot prayer, and J.J., six, the Adon Olam. It was a real treat for their father and for the entire congregation; it seemed to the boys as if the whole world was proud of them. On the following Sunday morning, their grandparents visited and gave each of the boys two dollars for doing such a fine job. When the boys told Deborah, then eight, that they each had been given two dollars, she complained that it wasn't fair. At which point, Moshe retorted, with the biting honesty of a ten year old, 'Well, so what, you can't even do anything in the synagogue!' Click click, I thought to myself, another woman radicalized.

"Oddly enough, until that moment, it never had occurred to me that it could or should be otherwise, that perhaps it wasn't fair to a little girl. Even more astounding was the fact that with all the weeks of secret practice, all the fuss I had made over the boys beforehand, and all the compliments they received afterwards, Deborah never once had complained. It was only the two dollars that finally got to her; to everything else she had already been conditioned…to expect nothing."

The same can be said for girls and women in my church, the Roman Catholic Church, and the Christian fundamentalists and Islamic faith. As a Roman Catholic woman, I grew up in a culture that made no secret that God preferred men to women. Still today, woman can't be priests. My two daughters, Kate and Elizabeth, are 26 and 24. These two beautiful, strong, educated Catholic women find no room in their church for them. Sexism in any form will not be sanctioned by these two women. I am proud that my daughters have a sense of honor. They know there is only one road to human rights, and that is total equality for women at God's altar and only then will it happen at the table of life. My daughters and their daughters to come will not be denied basic rights and freedoms by the Catholic hierarchy, rights and freedoms which have already have been bestowed on them by God. My daughters were born with human rights and if they are not realized than they will rebel.

Even Billy - Another great story and example that, still today, we do not accept women equal to men at God's altar is about a man I greatly admire, an American icon, the Rev. Billy Graham. I really like this gentleman even though I don't agree with all his interpretations of the word of God. He is kind, gentle, good, and forgiving. I believe the Holy Spirit is very much within this man. To watch and listen to Billy Graham is reassuring and soothing that not all fundamentalists are mean-spirited, judgmental people. What is sad, but true, about the legacy of Billy Graham is he has given a clear message to America and his own family that women are second-class in the eyes of God. Billy and Ruth Graham had three daughters born first. Yes, a succession of three daughters before producing a son, William Franklin Graham III. Yes, a son, a boy, a man-child to walk in his father's footsteps. The three daughters, Gigi, Anne, and Ruth had no such honor, no such privilege. They were girls, women, females; they had no birthright equal to the son born to Billy and Ruth Graham.

Anne Graham Lotz, the second daughter born to the Grahams, was a noted inspirational speaker and long considered the child who had inherited the greatest share of Billy's gift. It mattered not, however, for she was the wrong gender, she was not a man, but a woman. She could never be her father's successor. She could be smarter, wiser, and filled with the Holy Spirit but she is not a man, the male child would inherit the family business.

There is No Authentic Sexism

The oppression and second-class status of women rooted in theology is not supported by the bible or the word of God. There is no authentic sexism. Men just made it up and women bought it hook, line, and sinker.

There are three reasons based on the male interpretation of the bible for the continued second-class status of women in the world's religions.

1) Adam and Eve, the creation and the fall story
2) The 12 apostles were men
3) Saint Paul

Adam and Eve - When I read about Adam and Eve – the creation story – my interpretation is different from that of most men. I think God saved the best for last, and man was not complete, the world was not complete, without women. "Everything God created was supremely good." God's work was complete with the creation of women.

"Adam" is the Hebrew word for man. "Eve" is derived from the Hebrew word meaning life-giving. Wow! Eve means life giving. Now that's power!

As far as the fall story, I talked about this at length in an earlier section of this book. I believe Eve took responsibility for sin and Adam refused and pointed his finger at God and blamed God and Eve for sin. God was shocked and knew Adam wanted to be in control (that is, be master) over God and women. This was the big sin.

The Twelve Apostles - To say there were only 12 apostles and to say they were men is nonsense. The first apostles were women and the most faithful apostles were women. The life and resurrection of Jesus Christ survived because the women had courage and faith, not the men. Of course, I talk about this subject throughout most of the book (see "God's New Covenant..."). The men forsook Him while the women stood by Him.

Paul of Tarsus - Paul is perhaps the most damaging. St. Paul woke up one day and decided that women did not belong in The Church. Suddenly Jesus' full inclusion of women – and the fact that Jesus was who He was *because* of a woman – did not matter. Paul of Tarsus was favored over Jesus Christ when it came to the status of women. St. Paul may have loved Jesus Christ but he had a major character flaw and was fighting his own demons. To me, St. Paul lost most of his credibility on most matters when he, *not God*, decided to exclude women.

Salvation - Here are three reasons why women are the anointed, the chosen, the salvation of all human souls:

1) Eve took responsibility, Adam did not. "Her seed, their heel."
2) The first apostles were women, Mary of Nazareth and Elizabeth. They were one with the Holy Spirit. Later, Mary Magdalene was the faithful apostle. The men forsook Him.
3) Jesus believed in the full inclusion of women. Jesus had a wholesome, loving relationship with women. Jesus put His full trust in women, first His mother, and then Mary Magdalene. Jesus trusted Mary to go and evangelize. Go and tell the good news.

And the truth will set us free.

    This is a beautiful poem that speaks to the death of a child, being greeted by the feminine and human face of God, being greeted by forgiveness and redemption.

One Mother

Mary!

    I'm quite alone in all the world,
Into such bright sharp pain of anguish hurled
I cannot pray wise comfortable things;
Death's plunged me deep in hell, and given me wings
For terrible strange vastnesses; no hand
In all this empty spirit-driven space; I stand
Alone, and whimpering in my soul. I plod
Among wild stars, and hide my face from God.
God frightens me. He's strange. I know him not.
And all my usual prayers I have forgot:
But you –you had a son- I remember now!
You are not Mary of the virgin brow!

You agonized for Jesus! You went down

Into the ugly depths for him. Your crown

Is my crown! I've seen you in the street,

Begging your way for broken bread and meat:

I've seen you in trams, in shops, among old faces,

Young eyes, brave lips, broad backs, in all the places

Where women work, and weep, in pain, in pride.

Your hands were gnarled that held him when he died!

Not the fair hands that painters give you, white

And slim. You never had such hands: night

And day you labored, night and day, from child

To woman. You were never soft and mild.

But strong-limbered, patient, brown-skinned from the sun,

Deep-bosomed, brave-eyed, holy, holy One!

I know you now! I seek you, Mary! Spread

You compassionate skirts! I bring to you my dead!

You'll know him when you see him: first of all

Because he'll smile that way he did when he was small;

And then his eyes! They never changed from blue

To duller gray, as other children's do,

But like his childish dreams he kept his eyes

Vivid, and deeply clear, and visions wise.

See for him, Mary! Bright among the ghosts

Of other women's sons he'll star those hosts

Of shining boys! (He always toped his class

At school!) Lean forward, Mary, as they pass,

And touch him! When you see his eyes you'll weep

And this him your own Jesus! Let him sleep

In your deep bosom, Mary, then you'll see

His lashes, how they curl, so childishly

You'll weep again, and rock him on your heart

As I did once, that night we had to part.

He'll come to you all bloody and bemired,

And very shy. If he'd come home to me

I wouldn't ask the neighbors in to tea…

He always hated crowds…I'd let him be….

And then perhaps you'll take him by the hand

And comfort him from fear when he must stand

Before God's dreadful throne; then, will you call

That boy whose bullet made my darling fall,

And take him by the other hand, and say…

"O God, whose Son the hands of men did slay,

These are Thy children who do take away

    The sins of the world…"

                -Irene Rutherford McLeod